2-58
25

Glasgow
at the Crossroads

Alan Knight

Text and photographs © Alan Knight, 2010.
First published in Scotland, United Kingdom, 2010,
by Stenlake Publishing Ltd
Telephone: 01290 551122
www.stenlake.co.uk

ISBN 9781840334968

The Barras, 1978
Previous: Anderston Quay, 1976

Foreword

These images of Glasgow are a series of photographs I took over the period 1976 to 1985, during visits when I lived away from Scotland. This is a document of my impressions of certain parts of the city, just as the politics of the UK made its significant shift to the right. I was quite young at the time, not long graduated from art college and taking my first steps towards an independent life. I started learning photography when I was 16, and thanks to my energy and enthusiasm for the medium I had gained a decent amount of knowledge by the time I began taking these photographs. In my early days as a photographer I became attracted to certain kinds of subject matter, and the many wanderings around my home city, irrespective of weather conditions, became a kind of discovery. It was fun to drop into cafés and listen to the conversations, take a trip across the River Clyde on the passenger ferry, meander through cemeteries, wastelands and condemned buildings, hang around the stalls in the Barras, or explore the high rise flats around the Gorbals, catching images along the way. People were generally friendly, or just merely curious. Sometimes the bolder folks would actually ask to have their picture taken, but other subjects were less enthusiastic, such as the Glesga polis who eyed me warily as I snapped away at them from a safe distance. Today I'd probably get arrested!

There were times, like on a stormy rain-lashed day in winter with the light beginning to fade, when the atmosphere on the streets was bleak and desolate, but holding my trusty 35mm Pentax SLR camera I felt exhilarated in a strange way, despite being drookit and chilled to the bone. It became interesting to take photographs in difficult conditions, both interior and exterior. I wanted to try and push the boundaries of the different film stocks available to me, so on occasions I increased the speed of the film, with some decent results. Glasgow's changeable weather gave me the chance to shoot in extremely unpredictable situations (all seasons rolled into 20 minutes!), which altered the lighting pretty dramatically and created a bit of a challenge.

I found myself drawn to the slum areas of the city, I think partly because I played football in many of these run-down districts during my school days and could reminisce about my 'fitba' times. I had played regularly for my school team and some amateur clubs in the Glasgow and East Kilbride region, and had dreamt of becoming a professional player. It never happened of course, but those experiences stayed with me. Taking the photographs, I became both repelled and fascinated by the conditions in these areas – perhaps I was interested in dereliction and decay, in a visual sense. Some parts of the city, like Blackhill and Dalmarnock, were a picture of devastation. I didn't see one single car in Blackhill, but witnessed a fair amount of demoralised looking people. I tried to imagine living there and was glad that I didn't. It struck me just how difficult and tough life could be for some Glaswegians. I was born and raised in the West End – Byres Road – which wasn't nearly so up-market then, but still had nowhere near the levels of deprivation associated with other suburbs around the city. All these years later in the twenty-first century, and despite economic improvements, parts of Glasgow still suffer from deprivation and poverty, and I find that sad and kind of ironic. It's true that much of Glasgow has changed; urban blight has decreased and the city's cultural profile has been elevated (the Garden Festival and City of Culture status took place a few years after these photographs were taken), but it's also a reality that polarisation in our society has increased.

In and around the docklands vicinity, the ease with which I could move freely around the quays, yards, cranes and sheds would be remarkable today. I had virtually full access to those areas – I literally just turned up and started roaming. Nowadays there would be heavy security, officious behaviour, maybe a touch of paranoia – perhaps a marker of the psychological changes that have taken place since then, and of the privatised, corporate world we live in today. Some locations, like Queen's Dock, were completely deserted; the quayside sheds empty – a ghost dock waiting silently for demolition. I would try to imagine the place at its zenith, when Glasgow was the hub of heavy industry, but I knew I was observing the slow, painful end of an era.

My trip to Govan shipyards was a great experience. The friendliness and co-operation of the employees were second to none. I recall being impressed by the atmosphere and dynamism of the yards, and felt excited and privileged to be a witness to this vast workshop of industrial activity. I was surrounded by organised chaos and giant metal monsters, while in the sheds the air was thick with acetylene fumes from the welders and some of the guys calling out to me, 'dae ah look gorgeous son?' or perhaps something a touch more salty. It was always in pure jest of course; the brilliant gallows humour of the city was in full flow.

I'm glad to have preserved and restored these images, and I feel a great satisfaction in donating this modest photographic contribution to Glasgow's social history. I hope that it brings to viewers some of the atmosphere and characteristics of the city as it journeyed - for better or worse - from the old era into the new.

Alan Knight, 2010

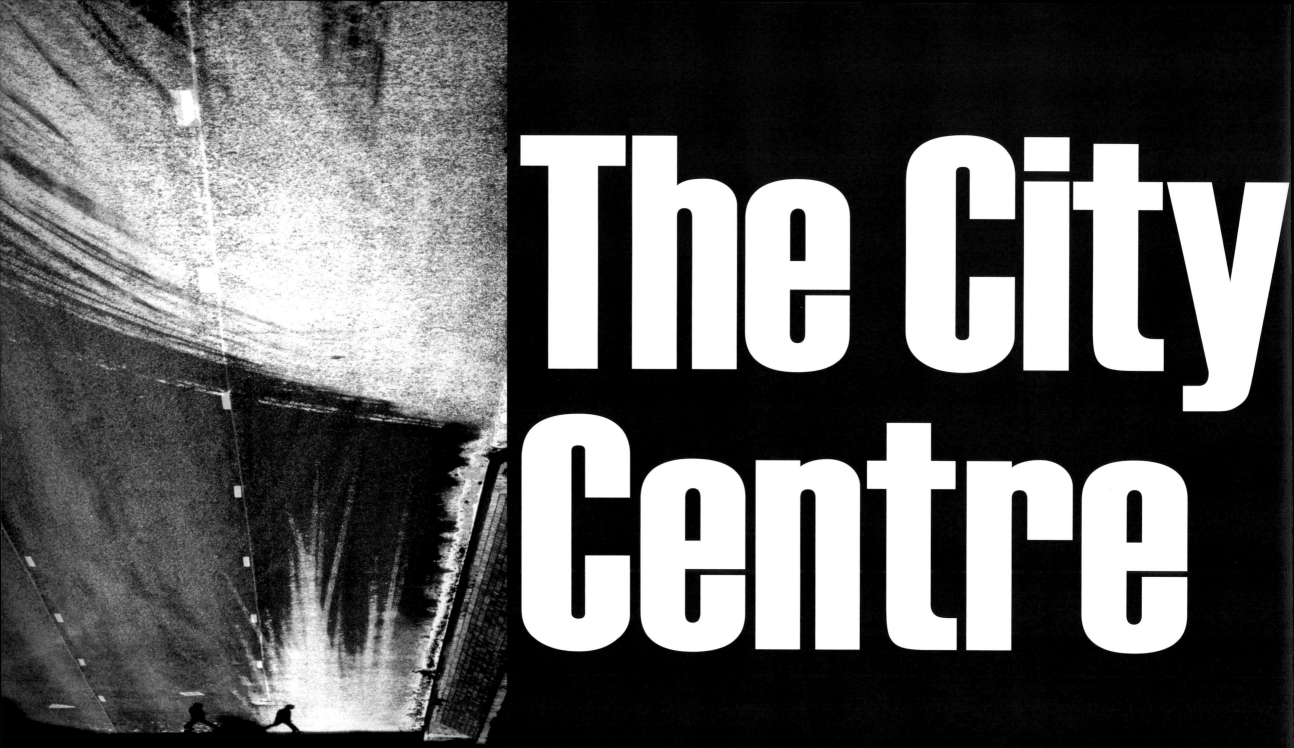

The City Centre

City Centre, 1976
(and next three pages)
Opposite: Charing Cross, 1984

City Centre, 1985

Buchanan Street, 1984

Buchanan Bus Station, 1984

Buchanan Bus Station, 1985
(and opposite)

East of the City Centre

Paddy's Market, 1984.

Calton, 1978
(and opposite)

Bridgeton, 1978
(and opposite)

London Road, 1984

The Barras, 1978
(and next five pages)

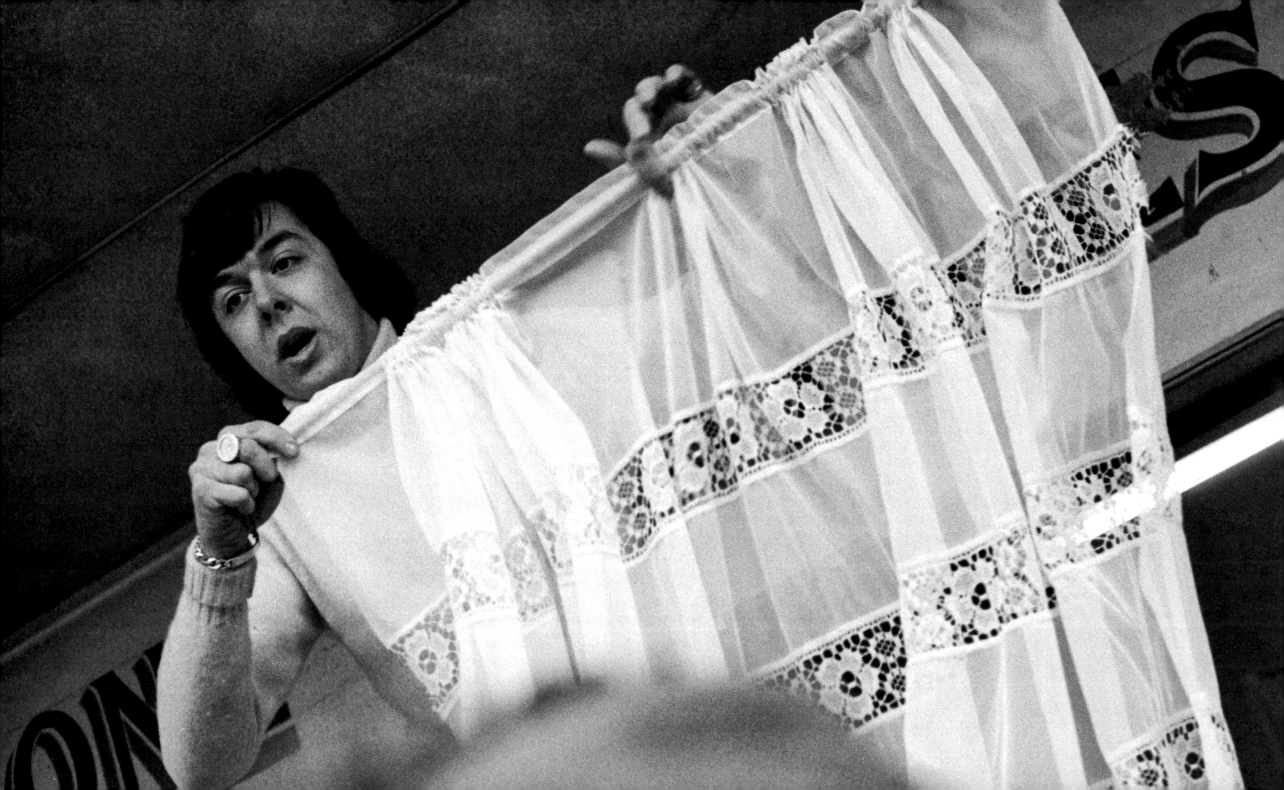

The Barras, 1984

Duke Street, 1984

Blackhill, 1979
(and next three pages)

Industrial estate near Blackhill, 1979

Dalmarnock, 1976
(and opposite)

Dalmarnock, 1978
(and next two pages)

South of the River Clyde

Mount Florida, 1977

The Gorbals, 1984
(and opposite)
Previous pages:
The Gorbals, 1978

Moffat Street, Hutchesontown, 1979

The Southern Necropolis, 1978

Castlemilk, 1984
(and opposite)

Kings Park, 1976

West of the City Centre

Botanic Gardens, 1984
(and opposite, left)
Previous: West End Café, 1985

Botanic Gardens, 1985

West End Café, 1978

West End Café, 1984

West End Café, 1985
Opposite: West End, 1976

Partick, 1984
Left: West End, 1985
Opposite: Hyndland, 1977

Partick, 1978

Partick, 1984
(and overleaf)

The River Clyde

Govan, 1977
(and previous)

Govan Shipyards, 1977
(and next 16 pages)

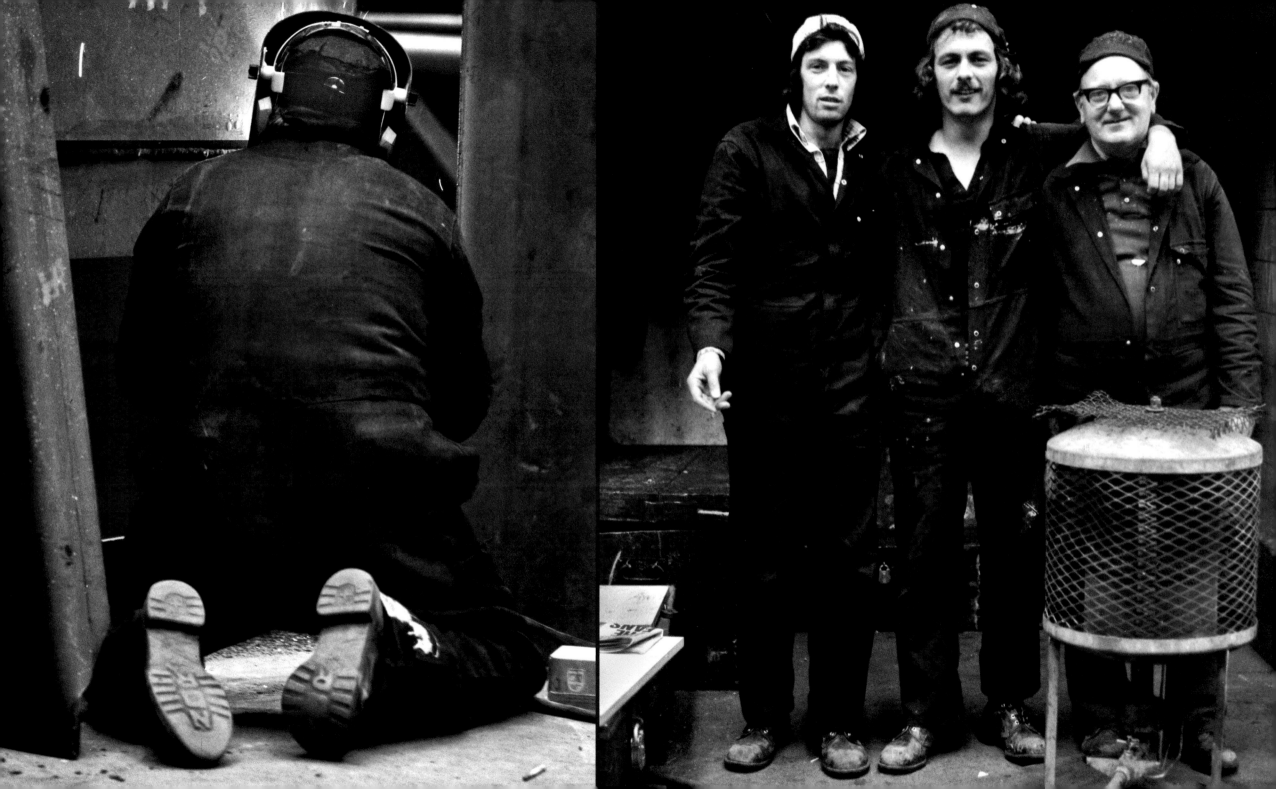

Govan Shipyards from Kelvinhaugh
Ferry Terminal, 1978

Tugboats, 1976

Tugboat crew,
Govan Dock, 1976

Princes Dock, 1977
Overleaf: Govan Graving Dock, 1979

Govan Dock, 1976
Right: Mavisbank Quay, 1976

Anderston Quay, 1976
Opposite: Car ferry terminus,
Lancefield Quay, 1976

The view from the north bank, 1977
Opposite: Finnieston Quay, 1977

Queen's Dock, 1979
Opposite: Stobcross Quay,
Queen's Dock, 1976

Kelvinhaugh Ferry Terminus, Ferry Road, 1979